# The Miracle of the Spring

Bob Chilcott

*for SATB and percussion*

Vocal score

MUSIC DEPARTMENT

OXFORD
UNIVERSITY PRESS

# OXFORD
## UNIVERSITY PRESS

Great Clarendon Street, Oxford OX2 6DP,
United Kingdom

Oxford University Press is a department of the University of Oxford.
It furthers the University's objective of excellence in research, scholarship,
and education by publishing worldwide. Oxford is a registered trade mark of
Oxford University Press in the UK and in certain other countries

© Oxford University Press 2015

Bob Chilcott has asserted his right under the Copyright, Designs
and Patents Act, 1988, to be identified as the Composer of this Work

Database right Oxford University Press (maker)

First published 2015

Impression: 1

ISBN 978-0-19-340062-7

Music and text origination by Andrew Jones
Printed in Great Britain on acid-free paper by
Halstan & Co. Ltd, Amersham, Bucks.

# Contents

# Composer's note

*The Miracle of the Spring* was written for Magdalen College School, Oxford, in 2014. The Director of Music, John Cullen, wanted a piece for choir and percussion instruments in the vein of my earlier work *The Making of the Drum*. I had read a poem by Charles Bennett, which I loved, on the subject of water, and I asked him to expand the idea into a suite of five poems, which ultimately make up the texts for this piece. The idea also reflected a conversation I'd had on a visit to the United States about the importance of water to all of us. In the cycle, I have used the glockenspiel and bell tree to depict the flow and sparkle of water, and a pair of log drums to reflect the dryness of the desert. The discovery of the spring at the end of the piece reminds us of the life-giving properties of water and how much we need to respect and value it as one of our greatest resources.

The percussion parts may be performed by members of the choir or separate percussionists.

Duration: *c.*12 minutes

# The Miracle of the Spring

Charles Bennett (b. 1954)

BOB CHILCOTT

## *1. Where water waits*

* Percussion 1: glockenspiel (or similar, e.g. metallophone) and log drums. Percussion 2: bell tree/mark tree and log drums. The part for log drums (movements 3 and 4) should be performed by both percussionists, using drums of different sizes/pitches. Separate percussion parts are available to download from www.oup.com.

6

## 2. The source of the spring

* Change from 'waits' to 'oo' at the beginning of the bar, maintaining a continuous sound.

strand-ed there._____ To - day I'll re-pair its hull___ and heal___ the gash where its

oo_____

oo_____

oo_____

**A. SOLO**

float-ing was bro-ken by a stone._____

**S.**

To - night I'll make an oar___ from a

**A.**

oo_____ To - night I'll make an oar___ from a

**T.**

oo_____ To - night_____ from a

**B.**

oo_____ To - night a

*p legato*

*p legato*

*p legato*

*p legato*

*p legato*

* Small notes = alternative line

I find the source of the spring.

-til in the end___ I find the source of the spring.

-til in the end___ I find the source of the spring.

in the end___ the source of the spring.

in the end___ the source of the spring.

# 3. To sing of water

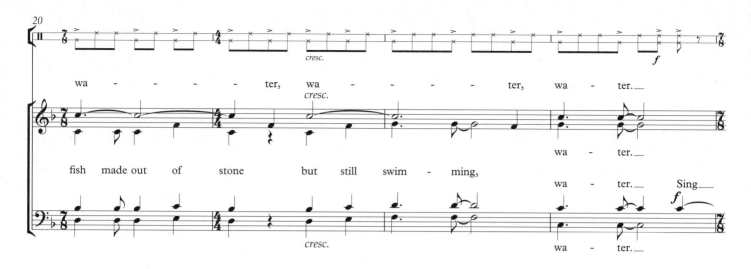

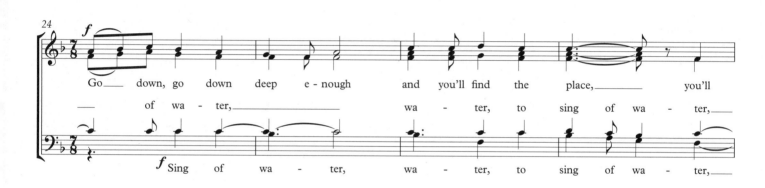

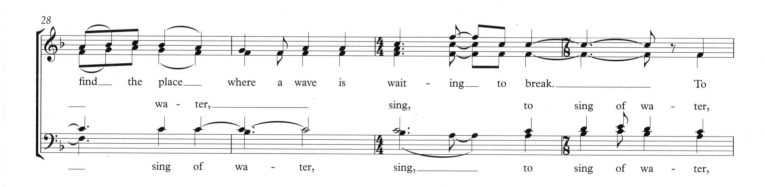

21

# 4. The desert

to the de - sert, de - sert.

In the de - sert, in the de - sert, in the de - sert,

**S. A.** in the de - sert, in the de - sert, in the de - sert, in the de - sert, in the de - sert,

**T.** in the de - sert, in the de - sert, in the de - sert, in the de - sert, in the de - sert,

**B.** I stayed in the de - sert be - cause I learned____ its name____

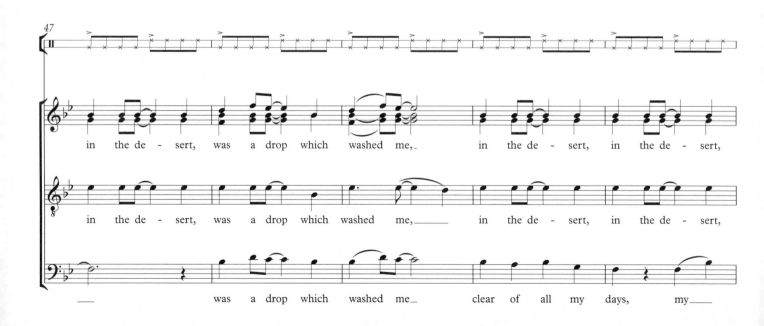

in the de - sert, was a drop which washed me,____ in the de - sert, in the de - sert,

in the de - sert, was a drop which washed me,____ in the de - sert, in the de - sert,

____ was a drop which washed me____ clear of all my days, my____

Perc. 1 to Glockenspiel
Perc. 2 to Bell Tree

in the de - sert, in the de - sert, in the de - sert, de - sert.

in the de - sert, in the de - sert, in the de - sert, de - sert.

days,_____ my_____ days, de - sert.

**Slower** ♩ = *c.*60

I be-came the de-sert be-cause I want-ed you to come_____ and

and

mm_____ mm_____ mm_____

**rit.**

let me show you what it means to drink,_____ to_____ drink,_____ drink.

mm_____ drink.

# 5. The voice of water